Animals with Armor

Crabs

by Julie Murray

Dash!
LEVELED READERS
An Imprint of Abdo Zoom • abdobooks.com

Level 1 – Beginning
Short and simple sentences with familiar words or patterns for children who are beginning to understand how letters and sounds go together.

Level 2 – Emerging
Longer words and sentences with more complex language patterns for readers who are practicing common words and letter sounds.

Level 3 – Transitional
More developed language and vocabulary for readers who are becoming more independent.

THIS BOOK CONTAINS RECYCLED MATERIALS

abdobooks.com

Published by Abdo Zoom, a division of ABDO, PO Box 398166, Minneapolis, Minnesota 55439. Copyright © 2022 by Abdo Consulting Group, Inc. International copyrights reserved in all countries. No part of this book may be reproduced in any form without written permission from the publisher. Dash!™ is a trademark and logo of Abdo Zoom.

Printed in the United States of America, North Mankato, Minnesota.
102021
012022

Photo Credits: iStock, Science Source, Shutterstock
Production Contributors: Kenny Abdo, Jennie Forsberg, Grace Hansen, John Hansen
Design Contributors: Candice Keimig, Neil Klinepier

Library of Congress Control Number: 2021940121

Publisher's Cataloging in Publication Data
Names: Murray, Julie, author.
Title: Crabs / by Julie Murray
Description: Minneapolis, Minnesota : Abdo Zoom, 2022 | Series: Animals with armor | Includes online resources and index.
Identifiers: ISBN 9781098226596 (lib. bdg.) | ISBN 9781644946558 (pbk.) | ISBN 9781098227432 (ebook) | ISBN 9781098227852 (Read-to-Me ebook)
Subjects: LCSH: Crabs--Juvenile literature. | Crustaceans--Juvenile literature. | Armored animals-Juvenile literature. | Animal defenses--Juvenile literature. | Veterinary anatomy--Juvenile literature.
Classification: DDC 595.3--dc23

Table of Contents

Crabs 4

More Facts 22

Glossary 23

Index 24

Online Resources 24

Crabs

4

Crabs are found throughout the ocean. They also live in fresh water. Some even live on land.

Many crabs can be found in **tropical** places.

Crabs have soft, flat bodies. Their bodies are covered by a hard shell. It is like armor. It protects them.

When crabs grow, their shells get too small. They grow new ones!

Crabs have two eyes. They often have **eyestalks**.

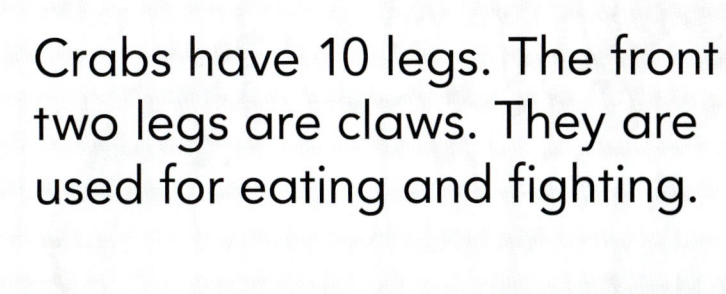

Crabs have 10 legs. The front two legs are claws. They are used for eating and fighting.

Crabs eat both plants and animals. They mainly eat **algae**.

Most crabs walk sideways. Some move forward and backward. Some can even swim.

Small crabs live for three to four years. Larger ones can live up to 100 years!

20

More Facts

- There are more than 6,700 **species** of crabs.

- The Japanese spider crab is the biggest species. It has a 12-foot (3.7 m) leg span!

- The pea crab is the smallest. It is about the size of a pea.

Glossary

algae – organisms that mainly live in the water and make their food the way plants do. They have no true leaves, roots, or stems.

eyestalk – a moveable body part that has an eye near its tip. It is common mainly in crabs, shrimps, and some other animals.

species – a group of living things that look alike and can have young together.

tropical – relating to regions located just north or south of the equator. Tropical places are known for being warm and humid.

Index

body 8, 10

claws 15

eyes 12

eyestalk 12

food 16

habitat 5, 7

legs 15

movement 19

shell 8, 10

size 20

Online Resources

To learn more about crabs, please visit **abdobooklinks.com** or scan this QR code. These links are routinely monitored and updated to provide the most current information available.